YES YOU CAN SERIES

EVOCATION

EVOKE THE POWER OF INTER-DIMENSIONAL BEINGS AND SUMMON SPIRITS

MARIA D' ANDREA

YES YOU CAN SERIES

EVOCATION
Evoke the Power of Inter-dimensional Beings And Summon Spirits

By Maria D'Andrea, MsD, D.D., DRH

INNER LIGHT/GLOBAL COMMUNICATIONS

YES YOU CAN SERIES

EVOCATION

**Evoke the Power of Inter-dimensional Beings
And Summon Spirits
By Maria D'Andrea, MsD, D.D., DRH**

© **2016 Maria D'Andrea**

Published by Timothy Green Beckley

DBA Inner Light/Global Communications - All Rights Reserved

Printed in the United States of America

Non-Fiction

Timothy Green Beckley: Editorial Director

Carol Ann Rodriguez: Publishers Assistant

Editor & Graphics: Tim R. Swartz

Sean Casteel: Associate Editor

William Kern: Associate Editor

Email: mrufo8@hotmail.com

www.ConspiracyJournal.Com

EVOCATION

Contents

DEDICATION

To both of my inventive sons:

Rick Holecek and Rob D'Andrea

They are both very supportive in all of my endeavors; they are adventurous, spiritual in their own right and a true Blessing to me.

FOREWORD
By
Robert D'Andrea

THIS book is the perfect guide on how to summon spirits in the "right way." I cannot emphasize how important it is to know what you're doing when dealing with spirits. If not done correctly you can open yourself up and be vulnerable to negativity, which is why this book is so essential if you are even contemplating interacting with spirits. Maria D'Andrea is my mother and has taught me so much, and I have continued to learn from her for over 37 years. I'm excited that she is able to share her knowledge on this subject with all of you. This is a book that you will want to keep as a reference guide after you have read it.

EVOCATION

EVOCATION

<u>**HOW IT ALL STARTED**</u>

THROUGHOUT my life, I have always been connected to the Spiritual, Psychic and Paranormal Realms. One way or another, situations came up around me in those areas.

When I was six-years-old, my mother, Maria Berde, and a group of people escaped from Hungary during the Revolution. It was extremely difficult, as you can imagine, and very dangerous. At one point, they thought to turn back. They were at the end of their rope. My mother told me that I said we need to move forward because I was told God will take care of us. So they kept going, and we were safe without any incidents and landed in Austria without a problem.

My father, Lichtig Laszlo, was always psychic, and, on my mother's side of the family, both my grandparents were also. My grandfather received much of his information from his older brother who had passed away.

At one point, when my mother was about 8-9 years old, she became very ill and nothing medical could save her. They were told it was just a matter of time before she would pass away and just to make her comfortable.

My grandparents and a woman they'd done a séance with in the past sat around a table and "called in" for help. They were told what herbs to give her and how to blend them. My mother recovered 100%.

They were also told at the time that she would go to a different country and, when in school, she needs to learn English. Obviously at age 8-9, that didn't make any sense.

EVOCATION

But when in college, she took English, and here we are. She was the only one who could speak the language when we came to America.

Psychic ability has always been a natural part of our family.

Both my sons, Rick Holecek and Rob D'Andrea, are very psychic and do readings as well as being equally analytical. My family has always had a balance of both. They have all been in some form of an analytical business.

I have been in my fields all of my life and professionally since the age of 16. It is a way of life. I ONLY do POSITIVE because I truly believe what we put out comes back to us. Good, bad or indifferent.

Even though I have always done readings, I love teaching people and speaking internationally on how people can do things for themselves in the Spiritual/Psychic/Metaphysical (Paranormal) Fields.

We still teach "underground" because of the power and we do not help negative people to gain these higher levels.

This is taught Master to Initiate (student).

I've written this series of books because I truly believe everyone has psychic/metaphysical abilities. This is why I teach these fields in classes and individually. That doesn't mean everyone is meant to work with it. Everyone is on their own Path that is correct for them.

The more you can do for yourself, the better...

EVOCATION

THE DARK SIDE OF SPIRITS

THERE are several stories I can tell you from personal experience. These are just a few to give you an idea of how situations are at times.

The Haunting On The Hill

I was called to a big house on a hill one day. It seemed that the residents moved in a few years prior and slowly everything was going wrong. They felt there was a negative spirit in the house and that it wasn't leaving. They were now at the end of their rope.

They had called a few people before me to remedy the situation, but nothing seemed to work.

When I first go into a situation like this, I check to see if there really is a spirit present or not. Not to be negative about it, but sometimes it's just that people have problems and want to blame anyone or anything other than themselves. Some people don't want to take responsibility for themselves. In which case I explain there's nothing there. They usually don't believe me. But I ethically can't do "work" when there's nothing there.

EVOCATION

In this case, there was a negative female spirit that was angry and depressed. She felt like dark energy.

I asked the people who lived there what made them think they had a spirit in the house. They proceeded to tell me that they had a teenage son who seemed to slowly get more and more depressed for no apparent reason.

Also, they would go into a room and all of a sudden feel "down" until they came out of the room. It was confusing to them because it wasn't always the same room.

I summoned the spirit. It seemed that she died and had a son she left behind. First she felt sad because she felt she deserted him when he still needed her. He was around 6 years old when she passed.

Then she became angry through time and resented being taken away when she felt she was still needed.

She wasn't attached to this house. She never lived in it. She did, however, live on that land before the house was built.

It took long hours to get her to finally understand she had no place here and that if she moved on, she might get to see her son. She put up a fight until she understood she didn't have a choice.

Once she moved on, I cleansed the whole house, one room at a time, to make sure she couldn't come back.

The last I heard, they didn't have any more problems and the son was back to his normal ways and doing well.

EVOCATION

The Spirits In The Basement

I relocated to an apartment in the town of Mineola, on Long Island in New York, a few years back. It was the bottom half of a house.

It was a great apartment, redone so it looked new and it came with a full basement, the length of the house. My son, Rob, moved with me at the time, to help me out. I was very happy we found it.

We were looking for a place for a while and nothing felt right. We came close, but it wasn't the right feeling. When we entered this place the first time, my immediate thought was: "This is home." We immediately took it. I excitedly called my other son, Rick, to say we were on the move and very excited.

We went to the basement and it was spacious, so perfect for storage and a washer and dryer.

I kept feeling I was not alone every time I went downstairs. It wasn't uncomfortable but it became annoying.

One day, I got fed up and decided to summon whoever or whatever was there and find out what was happening.

So I prepared and went down to the basement to do an evocation. It turned out that there were two spirits living there.

One was a heavyset lady dressed in clothes from the colonial time. She seemed unaware of her surroundings and was just wandering around.

EVOCATION

The other was a friendly, but very upset, spirit of a man from the prohibition time.

There didn't seem to be much interaction between them.

First, I dealt with the lady. She didn't know where she was or that she had died. Once I explained the situation to her, it turned out she wanted to move on but didn't know how. I helped her and she left. I felt very good about her.

Next, I focused on the man. The first thing he "said" was that he was happy the fat woman left because she annoyed him. Not a nice way to describe her, although true. I would have thought he would be happy he had company.

When commanded, he told his story to me. It seemed that he was happy someone could see him. I offered to help him move on also, but it upset him very much and he refused. I told him I wanted to know why he was so opposed to moving to his rightful place.

This was his story:

During the time of prohibition, he was in a speakeasy with a young lady he cared about on his lap. He was drinking and laughing with her, listening to the music and having a great time.

Then, all of a sudden, a rival gang broke in and shot and killed everyone, including, of course, the young lady and him. It was a very bloody scene and, as he was describing it, I could "see" it happening. This is one of the difficult situations we deal with at times.

EVOCATION

All he wanted to know was if the young lady was doing alright and if she was in a good place. He clearly was worried about her and had deep feelings since that was his only concern. I checked for him and told him she was in a better place and was happy and didn't hold any negative/bad feelings toward him. This seemed to relieve him. I still didn't understand why he didn't want to move on.

He then told me that he was afraid to move on because he was sure he was going to hell. I asked why. His answer was that it was his gang's fault that everyone died. It seemed that the rival gang attacked because he (with his gang) went to their place first and killed many people so the rival gang came to retaliate. He was upset about how many people he killed and without having any remorse at the time.

I explained about forgiveness and about how the Law of Grace works, but he refused to go. The fear was too strong. So he stayed in the basement. I made sure that if/whenever he decided to leave, he could do so.

Every time after that when I went to the basement he would speak to me or I would feel his presence if he didn't feel like talking. We had an understanding. I looked forward to seeing him. It felt positive. He wasn't negative or hurting anyone. The last time I saw him before I moved again, he still was not ready to move on. He now had a choice,

though. So he's either gone or still there and happy that his young lady was fine.

EVOCATION

<u>The Battlefield</u>

I was taking a walk at a battlefield in Virginia while on vacation. I was looking at the old houses where people used to live during the Civil War.

They even had a reenactment of a battle that everyone thought was very entertaining. The actors were very good.

I, however, did not feel the same way. Although I agreed about the actors, I was affected differently.

When I went on the battleground, I immediately felt sick to my stomach and became dizzy. As I looked around, I noticed a couple near me who also looked a little ill, and they walked away.

Now, as I was watching the "battle," I became aware that some of the actors were very angry and very bloody. They seemed to run toward each other and then all of a sudden disappear.

They would again run toward each other from the same spot, looking even angrier, and then disappear again at the same point as the last time.

As I watched, it was as though a film kept repeating again and again. I kept thinking, doesn't anyone else find it strange?

I then realized the others were not seeing the same thing. When the reenactment was over, everyone cheered. They set off a cannon and the crowd dispersed.

As I watched, the battle was still going on with the spirits of the fallen. I waited till I was more or less alone and spoke to them. Some ignored me, but a few came to listen. By the way, that can be a little unnerving if you aren't prepared for it.

After some time, a very few chose to pass on to the Higher Plane. Others just went back to the "battle."

I reminded them to be aware not to make people feel sick from their energy, but you can only do so much.

The last I saw of them, they were still doing "battle." Without having the time and the privacy to help, we can only do the best we can.

They are not harming anyone. Some people who are more sensitive may find they don't feel that great in a certain location or that they just don't like being somewhere but don't know why.

EVOCATION

EVOCATION

EVOCATION

***** Evocation is often confused with invocation. They are two different fields.

Invocation

This word means "to call upon." It is a ritual which is performed by someone trained in magick. Invocation aids in situations when the magician can't do it alone.

The magician <u>calls down INTO</u> herself/himself different beings to perform deeds or to get answers to questions or for psychic information. This spirit, deity, angel, archangel, inter-dimensional being, otherworldly being or other entity can also counsel or give advice to a person or tribe/village.

You would need to also have a shift in your consciousness to connect.

To "call in," some forms to utilize are: ritual, incantation, drums, formulae, amulets, talisman, dancing and other modalities.

I personally did not feel comfortable with this technique because I do not like to give up 100% control. There are other ways to achieve your goal.

EVOCATION

This is a technique utilized by trance mediums, as an example. Years ago, I was doing readings and paranormal work for several weeks. And as I was doing a reading, I slipped into an invocation form. I felt I was in a gray room but I didn't see a floor or any walls. It was comfortable, though.

And I was thinking about several things: what I'm doing later, different situations, etc. And at some point I realized I was hearing a voice "in the front of the room," but I wasn't interested and went back to my thoughts. After a while, I heard this person say something (I don't remember what) and I thought, "That is the stupidest thing I have ever heard." As soon as I thought that, I realized it was me speaking! As soon as I had that thought, I came out of it. I was still speaking to my client. I looked at her in case she saw my head spin or something.

Apparently, nothing out of the ordinary happened from her viewpoint. There was someone intuitive near me during the Reading and he asked me after where I "went." It wasn't a bad experience, and I've done trance work since, but there are other magickal modalities that work just as well and are safer.

Evocation

On the other hand, evocation gives *you* 100% control and you do *not* get hurt if you know what you are doing and use spiritual protection. Protection is VITAL!

Evocation is often misunderstood because of the media and negative magicians. They can summon evil spirits or positive spirits. The magician/practitioner is positive or negative. Magicians/people work from who they are. There is an occult law that states, "Like attracts like." Positive people attract positive friends and do positive work. Negative people attract negative friends and do negative work.

We Only Do Positive At All Times

In Evocation, we summon a spirit, deity, angel, archangel, inter-dimensional being, or whoever you intend to work with from the etheric plane.

This is ceremonial magick. Some utilize magickal tools such as wands or swords.

The DIFFERENCE is that the entity <u>CANNOT COME INTO</u> you. You use powerful ritual to call a spirit <u>to you</u>, NOT **in**<u>to you.</u>

You set up a barrier they cannot pass through to gain access to you or those with you. You take 100% control.

You <u>CANNOT </u>be possessed/taken over in an evocation. Make sure you follow the instructions.

Rituals can be very complex, but not the ones in my book. I want you to be able to do evocation and do it safely.

EVOCATION

MAGICK

MAGICK is an art and a science. We are the oldest science. They are both cause and effect. If we try a formula and it doesn't work, we don't repeat it (and don't need to tell people we tried.)

As I said in my book "Secret Magical Elixirs Of Life": Magick is the practice of causing changes through the use of power not defined by science.

If the formula works and you repeat it several times and each time it has the same outcome, then you can pass it on. As long as others stick to the exact same formula, it will work. If they "adjust" it, it probably will not. It is the same as a recipe. If your grandmother made a fantastic dish and everyone loved it, she will pass it on. If it stays exactly the same as it is being cooked and uses the same ingredients, it will have the same delicious outcome. On the other hand, if someone decides to update it, then probably not.

Therefore, we know the ancient spells, modalities and magick art work. Chemistry came out of alchemy and physics was born in metaphysics. And so it goes...

The word magick also means the great art and religion. It helps you to consciously connect to nature, the etheric planes, various frequencies, vibrations, electromagnetic fields, and the astral plane. It develops will power and tunes you into the spiritual and psychic realm by utilizing the ability over time (the more often you work with it, the faster you develop), and aids in psychically connecting to various energetic patterns.

Two Laws of Magick Are:

1-"As above, so below."

2-"Respect nature and have control over it."

3- I add: "Harm no one" and do "only positively"

- We really look at it as we understand the Laws of Nature and work <u>with</u> them.

We have all done magick without being aware that we were doing so.

Part of magick is will power and intent.

At some point, you have focused your intent on a set goal. You worked on it in the mundane world, but you also visualized it, anticipated it, and eventually it became real. That is working on both realities. You have now done magick.

As we work with magick and psychic ability more and more, it moves us up to a Higher Plane of Consciousness.

Every culture from ages ago have worked and demonstrated magick to help themselves, others and society.

EVOCATION

When you look at archeology, you'll notice they found cave drawings of people dowsing, showing worship, and throwing bones for guidance. Our ancestors were tuned into nature for survival. They depended on their instincts (psychic information) and on us as shamans and magicians to help in directing a better Path in their personal lives and the tribe's lives. Curiosity and drive helps us to evolve.

All cultures had this connection and, remember, they didn't have planes, trains and ships to connect to each other to learn about magick.

Magicians need to come forth. They are the ones who do magick, which also became known as science. They are the ones that through their "work" elevated themselves and society, one rung at a time, for those open to ascending their Path right now. We are walking the Pathways toward the unknown.

We are expanding into outer and inner worlds. WE are the explorers of time, space and other realms.

We look at it much like the Native American concept. Think of it as a spider web. On each strand, there is a human soul. All souls are on this web. If one soul does anything (good, bad, or indifferent), the whole web shakes. Energetically we are all connected.

Knowing this, we can tap into the energy streams in various situations and realms to take action.

EVOCATION

EVOCATION

__THE INTER-DIMENSIONAL REALMS__

YES, it is all real. Spirits, inter-dimensional beings, elves, fairies, deities, gods, goddesses, angels, archangels and genii, among other beings, are with us.

Some have always been here. Whether we see them or not, they still exist.

Everything is energy. Some are at different vibrational levels and frequencies than others. If you look at the difference between us and a table, the difference is the rate of vibration per second.

I always look at it as: we cannot see electricity but I am not putting my hand in the socket.

Then, there are those spirits and deities that we have created through time with our focus and beliefs. As an example, think of it this way:

There once was a tribe in the times of the caveman. They lived in a cave by the ocean. Between the cave and the ocean, there was a gigantic wall.

One day, a tidal wave appeared and everyone in the tribe thought they would die. As the gigantic wave came, it hit the wall and did not get to them.

EVOCATION

They started to worship the wall for saving them. Eventually, they gave it a name. Through time, their focus "built" a thought form/deity.

As the years went by, people down through the generations forgot the original reason for this and kept worshiping the deity.

Eventually, if anyone intuitive went by, they would psychically "see" this deity that was now energetically real. They had built a thought form.

Regardless of whether you believe in them or not, they still exist. You have the free will to decide if you will work with them or not.

When an entity comes to your call, most of the time you will see it with 3rd eye vision (psychic) if you are intuitive/psychic. The entity forms in the astral plane. Not physically, as most would have you believe. Others will not see this, although I've had sensitive people sometimes feel a presence or something in the room when I work.

We can contact various realms by knowing who we are summoning.

You cannot summon just any spirit or the procedure will not work correctly. You have preparation to do before embarking on this journey.

The reason you can summon entities from a different realm is due to the following:

You consciously decide what your intent is.

Next, you determine what form of spirit or connection would be of the most help. And then decide which you will summon by name.

EVOCATION

<u>YOUR SACRED WORKING SPACE</u>

MAKE no mistake that wherever you perform the evocation is Sacred Space.

You are working with Divine Universal energies. You are opening a doorway or portal into different Realms on the etheric, energetic planes.

Now, when I say this is Sacred Space, I don't mean as in a formal religion. Even though I'm an interfaith minister and shaman, when we do this work, we are dealing with Universal energies and Laws. It doesn't matter who or what you believe in; we can all be on a different Path, but moving toward the same destination/Source.

When you are in your Sacred Space, it serves as an extra precaution when you are connecting to otherworldly beings, to inter-dimensional forces, the astral or any Realm other than our own.

Some realms are overlapping our world; some are different frequencies that we may connect to in other realms. If they are not in the visible world or within our hearing range, it doesn't mean they don't exist.

Just as dogs can hear sounds that we, as humans, aren't able to, so there are sound ranges we can tune into psychically but not through our physical sense of hearing. The sounds, visions, sights we are not able to connect to are still there and you will be surprised how varied and unlimited the universe really is.

We can access so many Realms already. You just have to practice until you have your intent, focus, control, will and a sense of expectation in place.

If you have a specific room you can use for just this purpose, it affords you the space to build Sacred/Holy energy through repeated magickal work. If you do not have a specific room you can allocate to magick, don't worry. Remember, ages ago, tribes moved about and they were outdoors performing magick with nature.

WE can do magick anywhere.

We Are The Magick

That being said, there are things we can do to make it better for magickal work, when possible. It is as though you are adding a battery charger.

If you have a room (one of my students cleared out a walk-in closet for this), you can set it up in several ways. You can use one form or mix several.

You can set up an altar. You can also set up an altar on a cloth (white or violet is good as a base). It can be stationary or on top of a dresser when you work, and when you are finished you can fold it up with whatever you place on it and put it in your drawer. You can place ritual objects near you or crystals, candles, incense or any other tools of magick you feel will aid you in your "work."

EVOCATION

Remember, you do not need any of these tools; it is strictly a preference on your part. Even though they work vibrationally, they can also help you to set the mood and your mind-set.

For evocation intents, *you* are magickal. You are the power, as long as you memorize all that you are doing in the evocation 100% and follow the directions exactly. Know that you are non-limited since we are all connected to our Source and are part of God/Source/Divine Power.

When you are summoning during the evocation, <u>you</u> are Sacred Space and the Lesser Pentagram Ritual will protect you and anyone around you.

Sacred Space is also a mindset. We as shamans and magicians carry this energy with us and within us wherever we are. It surrounds us and permeates through us.

As an example that's funny:

I was at a dance club. As I was coming off the dance floor for a minute, there was a gentleman dressed partly in Native American clothes sitting close by. He pointed at me and said very seriously "shaman."

So I said, "Oh, you are a shaman?"

He replied, "No, I am Chief Little Fox. *You* are a shaman".

We have since become friends. He's chief of the Matinecock tribe on Long Island, N.Y. He also makes fantastic Native American jewelry that's available on his website.

EVOCATION

The sacred energies are there for all to see, within us and surrounding us. This energy being "seen" or "felt" comes up frequently with me even when least expected. Intuitive and sensitive people will be able to spot us. That doesn't mean they will always tell us.

EVOCATION

THE KEY TO PROTECTION/BANISHING

WHEN you do a summoning, you have to be safe and in control. You not only are protecting yourself, but, if you have others in the room, you are also protecting them.

Make sure they know not to get up from their spot and not to speak during the evocation.

Protection is imperative even when you are summoning a positive source. If by accident you summon one that is not positive because you read somewhere that it is, and it was wrong, you will still be safe. You can be in danger without the protection. There are magicians that did not take the proper steps/precautions and are now in padded cells. (I'm just making a point.) I cannot stress enough how important this is.

This would be like going to war if you were not protected first.

Rituals are built up by energy, power, light, will power and knowledge. Doing the same motions, perhaps wearing the same clothes (hence, ritual garments), all have impact because the ritual energy permeates the clothes when repeatedly worn. Also, the motions tell the universal energies that this is what you are doing again and will add quickness and accuracy. You are constantly building the energy into yourself, the motions, your will and your tools (if any).

The way I've come to look at it is:

Like chess, the rituals have strategy.

Like war, you need to be protected.

Like school, you need the knowledge.

Like ministry, you need a positive "knowing."

Like lightning, you need power.

WARNING: You must guard against ego or self-inflation. That is the downfall of many a magician. They become entrapped in their own ego about their abilities. They feel important because they can summon a being to their aid. (Control.) Some then end up turning to the dark side. It seems more powerful but it is a slippery slope. Staying positive and aware brings higher rewards and abilities and raises your Higher Consciousness and gives you more power and control. Use your Inner Light.

Another danger is obsession. Some magicians, some well-known, became so obsessed they felt they needed to do evocation. Remember that if a spirit gives you information, it doesn't mean it is written in stone. Use your own common sense.

NEVER change your spiritual ethics.

Entities do not know everything automatically. You may be dealing with something they cannot do or don't know.

EVOCATION

Ask questions and be aware of what the answer is. Ask more than once in varied forms of the question. Ask the name of the entity you summoned. Do not automatically look at it as being definitely correct.

***Important to note: Think of it as if you were asking a friend or a professional person, such as a lawyer, for advice. YOU always are responsible for your actions and for your decisions. And what you move on or not. You are the one who has to live with your choices. On the etheric plane, they don't have time as we do, nor a physical body, and any consequences will only be yours.

Remember, you are a magician, a wizard. Through time, you will gain 2nd sight or feeling of the unseen. The true magician "knows" his or her own abilities. They have no reason to tell others about it.

If you think about people with real abilities, they are not talking about it. They do what they do and keep working on improving. An artist doesn't have to tell people he's good. His work speaks for him. He doesn't need to convince others. They will see it.

All magick works in conjunction with psychic energy. So we need to be safe and protect ourselves.

When you activate these energies, it is as though you sent out a beacon or homing device on the astral/etheric planes. Saying basically "Here I am." You don't know what is attracted to this pull. It can be a positive spirit, inter-dimensional being, entity, deity, or any number of unknown other beings. It can also be a negative entity. Not because you are one or the other, but because the energies are neutral; they are simply psychic energies.

EVOCATION

On the positive side, you still do not work with whatever/whoever comes in. You are working with a specific being that you have preplanned to summon by name.

On the negative side, you have those that we consider psychic vampires or little dark creatures that, when looked at from 3rd eye vision, look like they are trying to cling/hang on with claws to your aura. This is their way of feeding off energy. They cannot get to you nor harm you because of the protection around you.

There are those that just come to bask in the energies you radiate when you work magickally. They are happy to be there and will not bother you. After all, you are making them feel good.

You may sense or psychically "see" them or clairaudiently "hear" them. I am sure that at some point in your life you thought you saw something and, when looking again, there was nothing there. Or you might have heard something only to turn around and see that nobody was speaking to you. I find when I get clairaudient (psychic hearing) information, it sounds exactly the same in my head as someone verbally speaking to me. I have to consciously separate the two.

When my son, Rob, was in kindergarten, I went to the supermarket after leaving him at school. At the market, I "heard" him speak to me, so I turned around and answered him. Of course, nobody else heard him in the market aisle. He told me later he wanted to tell me something and he was very focused.

EVOCATION

My other son, Rick, was in the Navy and out at sea. I was focused on "calling" him psychically to have him call me to just catch up. I received a call eventually and he said he "heard" me but wasn't near a phone and after I "call" once, to please stop. He'll call on the phone as soon as he is able.

Oh well, live and learn.

They sometimes want to trick you by seeming positive when they are not. They also have, at times, looked like a relative when they are not.

The reason for this is so they can bask in the energy fields you are generating. When you utilize protection, this will not happen. And you are summoning a specific being, so even if you have other spirits on the OUTSIDE of your protective field, it does not matter.

When you summon, nothing can get to you, including the one you summoned. Everything is outside your protective field. You are safe.

If you have others around you when you are doing evocation, it is important to protect them as well yourself. FIRST...We always make sure they understand the dangers of going outside of the protected area and that they also understand that this is serious. You are contacting a different dimension. You need your focus. You cannot have someone around that thinks it's a joke or someone who is negative.

We do not have anyone with us when summoning who is a nonbeliever. We are keeping them safe and we do not need to convince or convert anyone. They are on the right Path for themselves. They will come to this awareness at some point in their lives or not. They are on the Path they are meant to be on. Trying to convince them is not only counterproductive but will turn them off.

Even though there are several forms of protection, the one we are using is the best one for evocation purposes and has been used consistently by magicians because of its power. Remember, if a powerful method works through time, and has proven itself, that is the technique we prefer. Why reinvent the wheel?

EVOCATION

<u>WORDS OF POWER</u>

ALL words have power. You don't always consciously think of it, but you've already used some in your life.

Think of a time when you gave a command. Such as, if you had a small child that was going to run across the street, you would've used a powerful, authoritative voice that was said as a command, not a request, when you said "stop." It would not have occurred to you that you were not going to be listened to.

At work, you might have made a decision to do a job a specific way and when asked about it (or being congratulated), you would have given a definite response without expecting to be questioned about it.

Now, think of a beautiful, peaceful place. See yourself being relaxed, enjoying yourself, without a care in the world. You feel the warmth of the sun on your face, you feel everything is in your favor, and you are deeply and fully happy and at peace.

At this time, pay attention to your body. You will notice that your body is peaceful and relaxed. You have done nothing physical. Nothing has changed in the last minute. You are responding to the power of "words." (Mental or verbal.)

Words not only mirror your thoughts, but words create your reality.

I had a very wonderful student, Robert, who for years when I first met him had a negative outlook. He would say things like: "Nothing good ever happens to me," and "I'm always unlucky."

Through time, as we worked together, slowly his outlook changed. He became more positive. People on his job started to talk to him more; he met a nice young lady because his change was noticeable and people related to him in a different way now.

He started to say "I am always lucky" as an exercise we did. He didn't believe it, but he kept saying it to himself and to others. Through time, as his vibration changed, because he was putting out the "word," he noticed he started to win things. He would win a jacket in a newspaper contest he entered. Then he would win stuffed toys at carnivals or money. He would give the toys to his nieces and nephews. Now he also started to believe in his good fortune.

Robert then started to win tickets to sports games and some lottery tickets occasionally paid off. He won movie tickets, theatre tickets, tickets to concerts and numerous other events. It became so frequent that in one day he won tickets to a concert, the theatre and a jacket. The theatre and concert tickets were for the same day, so he gave the theatre tickets to me since he wanted to go to the concert. He also through time gave away much of what he won.

Part of his luck was that he knew the universal laws. He always remembered to give back. That could be a toy, ticket or simply advice. And when he didn't win, he didn't complain. He looked at it as an opportunity for someone else who could use it more and consoled himself that he would win another time.

All this just because he changed the "words" in his mind.

People always said they didn't understand how he was always so lucky, but we know why...

We need to clean our spiritual/mental house. When you find yourself thinking a negative thought (we are, after all, human), quickly say (mentally or verbally) the word "cancel" and replace it with a positive opposite thought.

To be able to do magick, the essential quality you must have is the ability to control or change your thoughts while performing magick. Other qualities that are included are:

Creativity in thought, analytical thought, knowledge, detachment (which is a control of your consciousness), inner control and focus of will.

When you speak a word, it sends out an energy stream into the universe and all the realms to connect with what you are creating or what/who you are summoning. This thread does not have any barriers. Energy runs through everything and everyone. It is non-limited.

EVOCATION

You are, in essence, sending out a "call." You are at one end of the phone, what or who you seek is at the other, and the words are the line connecting you.

When we are doing evocation, we always do so verbally, thus adding the vibrational tone to shake up the universal energies to have a quicker, more controlled and more powerful outcome.

Your tone of voice (with authority) and your intent, among your other "tools" at the time, all have impact on the outcome.

Remember, the more you work with magick, the Higher you are elevating your own spiritual Path.

EVOCATION

YOUR OUTLOOK

YOUR outlook is a very important part of evocation, as well as with all magick.

You have to approach it with knowledge, protection, sincerity, positive intent, focus, will power and expectancy.

You gain knowledge, because without that tool, you cannot do evocation properly and you can get hurt. This is not a game to be played lightly. If you follow the directions from knowledge and memorize them by heart so that you do not have to think of what comes next, you cannot be in harm's way.

In other modalities, you can be in danger even if you are careful. Much depends on your abilities and your teacher. In evocation, you are perfectly safe.

As an example of knowledge and protection:

I knew a practitioner who never utilized any form of psychic self-defense. I kept warning him and offered to teach him my self-defense technique that I had created and that I can guarantee works. However, he didn't want to take the time and thought it wasn't that important since we can have free will control over spirit.

EVOCATION

A few years later, I found out he was in a mental institution because he couldn't tell the difference between the physical and etheric planes. They were all the same to him.

They really needed someone in our field to know what happened to him and help him out of that maze. Doctors do not understand and so cannot help much.

Eventually, he became better and went home. But by that time, he had lost his job and his family.

He is doing great since then, no problems. You need to be aware of the dangers. I always strongly recommend psychic self-defense for all other forms of magick and for when I or anyone else does a reading. That is why I always teach that as my first class.

Sincerity is also a base. We approach all with an open heart and sincerity. This is a vibrational energy that helps to set everything into motion.

A positive attitude is a must. We never do any negative work or have a negative outlook. Remember: "Like attracts like."

Your focus must never waver. Make sure you are set and know exactly what you will do prior to starting your evocation ritual. Without focus, how can you hit your target goal?

Will power is positive energy that keeps you on the move. If you have a goal in life, as an example, and you get sidetracked due to mundane things in your life getting in the way to slow you down, you will then utilize your will power to get back on track with your goal. You will notice that people who are successful in their personal or business lives all have strong will power. So it is with the evocation.

Expectancy is a major key. If you do not expect it to work, why even start? If you are going to TRY evocation to see if it works, it won't. You are already putting into motion the thoughts to cancel yourself out. What we think, we create.

We all know someone who will say, "I always have a headache." So if it happens that they do not have one, the Universe says, "Oh, I heard you always have a headache and I forgot to give you one yesterday. I'm so sorry. I will give you the headache you are waiting for today." And then they are surprised that they have another headache. Why are they surprised?

You have to KNOW you will succeed. Otherwise, you won't.

When a track runner goes to the Olympics to set a new record, he doesn't say, "Let me try." He thinks, "I know I can succeed." If he doesn't succeed, he says, "Okay, I will work harder on my goal and keep at it until I win."

He doesn't look at others. He says, "Nobody ran it in (this amount of time) before, but I will be the first one." It is amazing that once someone breaks a record, then others can also do so, because they are no longer confined by their own limited thoughts.

Your energy through time doing evocation, becomes Sacred Space/Holy energy. It is just as sacred as if you were in any other Holy location. You are the Sacred Space.

EVOCATION

It is important that you know that doing evocation not only brings you to a Higher Consciousness, but brings you closer to Divine Power.

Part of your outlook must be that we do not believe everything a spirit says. Always question. They are not all knowing.

EVOCATION

BANISHING TECHNIQUE/PROTECTION

YOU may not have a response right away when you evoke. Keep at it. Remember, you didn't just get on a bicycle the first time in your life and race a marathon cross country.

Before entering into the evocation ritual, do some meditation to tune into the alpha and theta brainwaves, to become a "seer" and to be able to connect on the other planes.

I have friends in the scientific community. We have been tested and it has been proven that our brainwaves change.

Your Brainwaves:

Gamma = this is our fight or flight level

Beta = this is our everyday/speaking to each other wave

Alpha = this is our intuitive/psychic wave

Theta = this wave is a deeper psychic wave

Delta = your deepest level, coma and yogis who stop their heartbeat

EVOCATION

Take the phone off the hook, shut off any noise around you, close the door so you are not disturbed or go outside in an area where nobody will bother or see you. You will need your focus and this is not the time to be taken off track. Later, when you are proficient, it will not matter if you are in Madison Square Garden...

This method is called by many names. The name I use is the "Lesser Pentagram."

Before you begin, you need to get rid of any negative energy that may be surrounding you. There are a few methods you can use. Pick whichever one you feel you resonate with.

Cleansing Energy Techniques:

1-You can do so by focusing on White Light coming from above your head, going down through you and around you into the earth, and focusing on all black, gray, negative energy flowing from and around you into the earth to then dissipate.

2-Think of all negative energy around and through you flowing through the bottom of your feet as energy streams. Next, visualize it streaming into the center of the earth, where there is a ball the size of a baseball that is the core of mother earth. "See" this stream wrapping around the ball to ground you and get rid of all negativity.

3-This is another technique you can utilize. Take a shower and focus on all the negativity around you and within you flowing down the drain along with the water. Give it a few minutes. You will know when you are done by feeling there isn't a need any more to stay.

If you are using special clothing, a cloak, the same shirt or blouse, as an example, this is the time you would put it on. This isn't necessary, but remember, what you wear, if the same each time, will retain and build energy.

If you are using a wand or sword, this is the time you take it out. You should note that I don't use a tool but use my arm/fist instead. It is your choice.

*Note: If you are utilizing a tool, such as a wand or ritual clothing, make sure it is cleansed of all negative energy before you work with it. The easiest way to proceed with this is to put your "tool" into direct sunlight for 3 days. This can be outside or on a windowsill or a dresser that has sunlight on it all day. This takes out any negative energy the tools may hold.

The cause can be that the maker of the wand was upset or having an off day, the material in the cloth could have been sewn by someone with a negative personality but great sewing ability, and so on. We are starting out with a clean slate where only your positive energy will be connected and resonate with your tools.

If you use your body, you can do the "work" anywhere. If you use a magickal tool, it becomes an extension of your body and you will be using that tool for the ritual from then on. That doesn't mean you cannot do the ritual without the sword or wand, just that you will be, in essence, programming yourself and the universe to expect it. You may not feel as comfortable without it if the situation arises at a later date. If you know ahead of time that you will be performing this ritual, of course, you can simply take your tools with you. Whatever is most comfortable for you will work the best for you.

Clear Your Thoughts of Negativity

You can do this in a number of ways. One such way is to focus mentally so that all negative thoughts are now under your control and must leave. They do not surface while you are doing the evocation until you are 100% finished and are back to your mundane/everyday life.

Next, focus for a minute on a positive thought that makes you happy, such as a person, vacation, something you've done or will do...

Will and Intent

Get very clear in your mind what your intent is. Focus on exactly what you are looking to achieve. Then focus your will power on this outcome and stay focused on what you are doing at all times.

Make sure that you memorize this ritual and know it by heart without having to think about what the next word or motion will be. Without doing this, you will not have the power nor the control to be able to do the evocation.

EVOCATION

Five Steps: *One Flows Into The Next*

Step 1:

1- Stand in the center of the circle you are working in. (It is not a physical circle that you have to draw.) It is in the center of the area you are protecting, which may include others in the room.

*When saying the words, it is done verbally and you must do so with conviction, authority, and as a command. This is not a request! Feel the words vibrate throughout your body and if using a magickal tool, throughout the tool, which an extension of your body. Feel the vibration expanding through to the ends of the universe to connect with you.

Step 2:

Forming the Cabalistic Cross.

1-Face the East, "see" or think of bright white light coming from above your head, into your forehead and out to the universe. Touch your forehead with your right index finger and say: **ATOR** (pronounced Ah-tah)

2-Next, visualize (or think) the bright light going down into the earth. Point down in front of your groin with your right index finger and say: **MALKUTH** (Mahl-koot)

3-Touch your right shoulder and visualize the white light from your chest going to the right. Touch your right shoulder and say: **VE-GEVURAH** (Vih-G'boo-rah)

4-Touch your left shoulder and visualize the light from your chest going to the left. Touch your left shoulder and say: **VE-GEDULAH** (Vih-G'doo-lah)

EVOCATION

5-Visualize all the energy tracks you created, and, clasping your hands together before your chest, say:

LE-OLAHM (Lih-oh-lahm) – **Amen**

Step 3:

1-Face the East. Visualize your right hand as powerful energy (or hold your wand or visualize a steel dagger in your right hand). With your right index finger, you will trace a brilliant blue light to form the banishing pentagram. (5 pointed star)

To trace the pentagram: Begin at the lower left, move up to the top center, down to the right, up to the side and to the left, across to the right side, then back to the point where you started.

<u>#1</u>

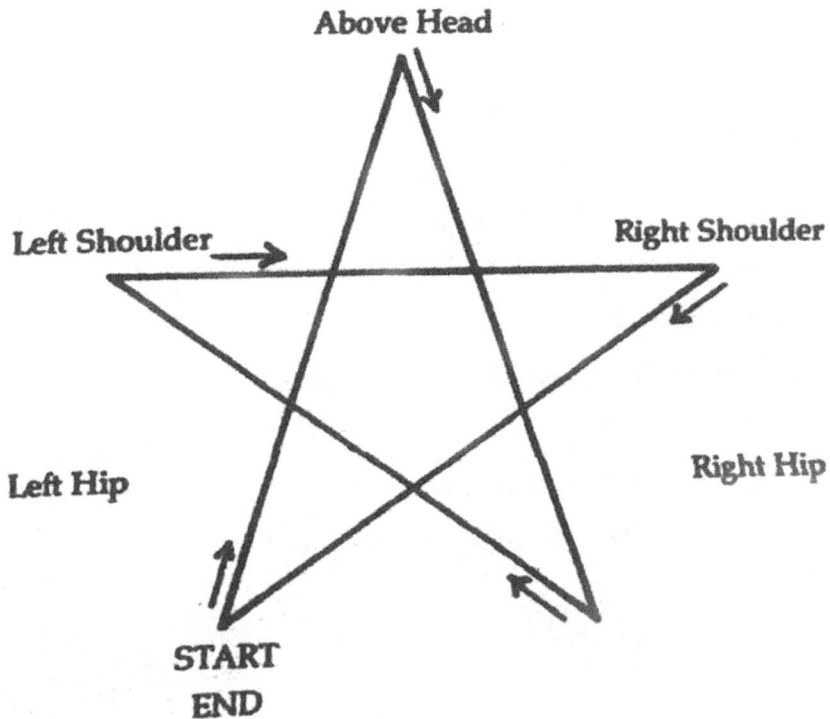

Above Head

Left Shoulder   Right Shoulder

Left Hip   Right Hip

START
END

EVOCATION

<u>1-</u>Point to the center of the pentagram; "see" brilliant red light flowing into your hand; make a fist and punch it with force with the red light into the center of the pentagram; and "see" it going out to the universe. With the same word power as the cross, say: **YHVH** (Yud-Heh-Vahv-Heh)

Start at the center of the star where you have your fist still through it; open your hand; pull in a line of brilliant white light at about chest height. Still holding out your arm, this line is pulled across in a clockwise direction at the edge of your circle to form your barrier. As you start to turn clockwise with the line, stop when you get to the South.

2-In the South, trace the pentagram in the same way and repeat the same gestures. When you "punch through," say: **ADNI** (Ah-doh-nye)

3-Turn to the West, trace the pentagram in the same way and repeat the same gestures. When you "punch through," say: **AHIH** (Eh-heh-yeh)

4-Trace the pentagram in the North the same way and repeat the same gestures. When you "punch through," say:

AGLA (Ah-glah)

5-Return the line to the East where you started.

Step 4:

Without moving from this spot, extend your arms out to the side at shoulder level to form a cross still facing the East. Visualize gigantic archangels as you say:

"Before me Raphael,   (Rah-fay-ehl)

EVOCATION

Behind me Gabriel,   (Gahb-ray-ehl)

On my right hand is Michael,   (Mih-chai-ehl)

On my left hand is Auriel. (Ohr-ree-ehl)

About me flames the Pentagram,

Within me shines the Six-Rayed Star."

Step 5:

Repeat the Cabalistic Cross.

Take your time to master this ritual so you are comfortable with it and do not have to think of the next step or words as you focus your intent and power.

Taking a little longer to get it right can mean all the difference in the world.

The meaning of these words are:

ATOR = Thou Art

MALKUTH = the Kingdom

VE-GEVURAH = and the power

VE-GEDULAH = and the glory

LE-OLAHM = forever Amen

Knowledge is always power.

******* There are techniques in which you do *not* need to do this ritual and you can, as my friend Rodney coined the acronym, IGD, because I am always saying – I Go Direct.

EVOCATION

HOWEVER: If you cannot do this ritual with control, you cannot move onto Higher Levels of power. This ritual gives you the ability and the protection you absolutely need to become a powerful and positive practitioner of magick.

Some knowledge can only be passed on Master to Initiate, such as in my Mystery School, **"The D'Andrea Institute of Esoteric Studies,"** because some of our ancient – as well as my original – formulae are still underground. Our ways are still not given out to negative people. Some of us only pass knowledge on this Path to positive people to gain Higher Levels for ourselves, each other, the planet and all on it.

A Mystery School teaches immutable laws dealing with the mind and nature. It teaches how we relate to the universe, the cosmos, the body and spirit. It teaches secret esoteric mysteries. Part of this knowledge is to take responsibility for all of your actions. Healing, psychic abilities and parapsychology/metaphysics are incorporated in these schools of knowledge.

Utilizing the Lesser Pentagram and other forms of positive magick/shamanism gives you not only the ability to do evocation/conjuring, but each time you do so, you are moving yourself up a notch within yourself to your Higher Consciousness.

This is a method that we KNOW works, with practice and patience.

Some shamans, magicians and others utilizing this ritual of power never switch from this technique. The outlook being: if it works, why fix it?

EVOCATION

EVOCATION

<u>CONJURING</u>

FIRST, you have to be aware that if you conjure a negative entity by mistake, you are perfectly SAFE.

It can only come outside of your protective field. It cannot enter, harm or upset you. You may "see" or "feel" it, but it *cannot* get to you.

It is important for you to be consciously aware of this, keep calm and command it to go forthwith back to whence it came NOW in the name and power of GOD.

You may have to repeat it three times, but it has to go by the third time. You have the control always. ALL WAYS.

Some may not understand why we command or speak with control. We would not do so with people, because that is negative and we don't try to counteract their free will.

However, this is not the case with otherworldly beings. WE, in the physical body, have free will. Non-physical beings do not have free will. They are coming to help us because it is in their nature.

Just, as in nature, there are predators. Which is why, when they attack, we aren't surprised. After all, this is their nature. So it is with these more positive beings; it is their nature to help when called upon.

They have different natures, just as with people. If someone is an expert at math, then that is not the one you call in for advice on love.   Awareness is important so that you know who/what you are calling in prior to starting. Remember, knowledge is important. Not just focus, but also will, power, expectancy and knowing.

They are waiting to be called so they can fulfill their Path. That doesn't mean they will not test you or that they perhaps won't come when you "call in," if you are doing so incorrectly. However, if you keep at it, you will learn, just as with anything else.

There are various versions of a conjuring. As new Masters/ magicians/shamans, we eventually develop our own methods that work, but always with the same base.

When we are summoning a non-corporeal being, we are helping them to do what is natural for them. I always have a funny picture in my mind of all these entities being in a long line, waiting to be summoned.

<u>Summoning Ritual</u>

The following is said as a Command, in a serious voice and with authority. It is preferable to state it loudly when it is opportune. Approach it with a positive heart, respect, authority, sincerity and love.

The following has a blank (_?____) to insert the name of the entity you are summoning.

EVOCATION

Remember, always, that you are in control when you conjure.

Now, say:

Hear me, Oh (_____), I now do summon thee. I am clothed in the power and name of the Supreme Majesty. I am armed. I conjure thee by the Him, who maketh the earth, the fire, air, water and ether. By the Holy names of God, I conjure thee: ADONAI, TZABAOTH, EL, ELOHI, SHADDAI, and TETRAGRAMATION. I command thee to come to me (us) instantly in a fair human form. I evoke thee by the power of the most High, by Divine Power, by the King of Kings.

I command thee with power, by Him who spake and it was done. I being made of God, being part of God, existing through the will of God, do conjure thee to come at this my call quickly and obediently.

I conjure thee (_____) in the powerful names of GOD as ADONAI, EL, and ELOHI. Come to me on the outside of the circle to do my bidding.

The universe and cosmos tremble at His power. Tremble the terrestrials, celestials, and on all the realms, known and unknown. I command (_____), come now swiftly, without delay from whatever part of the universe or realm thou are in.

I command thee to answer rationally all my questions. Come now peaceably and visibly without delay. Fulfill my commands of that which I desire. Unto the end of manifesting my interest. Speak to me clearly, understandably, intelligently and in a peaceful, calm manner.

EVOCATION

I conjure this command thus:

Appear before me outside the circle, I command thee, (_____), as it was spoken through the power of the Supreme Majesty.

So Be It!

If the spirit looks or feels frightening, Command it loudly: *I command thee. Show yourself in a fair human form, I command in the power and the names of ADONAI, EH-HEH-YEH!*

At the end of this book, there are some beings and their sigils/signs to help you to evoke some positive spirits.

Once you have complete control over what you are doing/speaking and you are comfortable doing evocation, then you can branch out into summoning various spirits and otherworldly beings.

***To be a true Master and to do your own rituals, you need to have knowledge and skill in the following areas: Science, creative mindset, literature, drama, sound vibrations (music, poetry, rhyming, rhythm, proper speech), herbs, stones, oils, candles, movement (dance is excellent for this), basic chemistry, cosmic concepts, psychic ability, basic drawing (for sigils, etc.), among other attributes. And a strong spiritual base.

WE as true Adepts on a Higher Level are the ones who can directly link our energies with different realms.

Remember that if you summon, by accident, a negative spirit, it cannot get to you. You have the control to banish it and it cannot penetrate your circle.

EVOCATION

You are a Divine Being. You are part of Divine Power and so have the control. *** NEVER let an entity tell you what to do or intimidate you. YOU have control always.

Questions Put to Spirit

Questioning the spirit/entity is of the utmost <u>importance</u>. You have to know who/what you are dealing with, that it is the one you summoned and it is not of the negative path.

It might have misconnected when you summoned, or it could have hitchhiked in the open door/portal when you did the summoning. Whatever the cause may be, you have to be sure you are connecting correctly.

You have to also be sure that the answers you receive are intelligent, that you understand them, and that they are the TRUTH.

Still, remember, that doesn't mean the spirit/entity is always accurate, so double-check. Phrase the questions in more than one form.

1-Ask as a command – What is your name?

If you get a name you do not know, remember sometimes they may have several names. Such as: Neptune and Poseidon are different names for the same God, the God of the Sea, just in different cultures. In this case, ask for the name you would understand.

If you do not receive an answer, say with authority:

By the Power of ADONAI, YUD-HEH-VAHV-HEH, I command you to tell me your true name/names without hesitation.

EVOCATION

At this point, you will be given the true name/names. It/they cannot lie to you.

When you get the name you summoned, you can go to the next step. If not, then command in a loud voice:

Spirit, I command you to leave and to go back from whence you came, in the name of the Highest Power, the King of Kings, God. Who, when He spoke, all trembled and obeyed. Depart NOW!

2- At this point, if the spirit/entity being is who you summoned and appears in a fair form, so as not to frighten, you can proceed to the acknowledgement.

Acknowledgment

At this time, you can acknowledge the spirit being present.

With authority and calm, say:

Oh, Great Spirit named (_____), I welcome you that you came to me through God, as I summoned you in the name of the Most High, GOD, ADONAI, who created all the universe and all the Realms. Under His protection and command, He is obeyed, and through His will I am obeyed. As I called, through this time you are to obey me and do my bidding without question, affably and in a fair form. You shall stay until I give permission for you to depart. You shall perform my commands with Truth. Through GOD I called thee. Answer my questions and do what I command for you to perform with no hesitation and agreeably.

EVOCATION

You can now start to ask the questions you planned before the summoning. Or state what you want the entity/spirit to do.

Be clear, concise and ask with authority. If you do not get an answer, repeat the previous command for the spirit to answer you. If it doesn't, remember the question has to be in the spirit's nature or it will not know the answer.

The entity has to know you are in control.

It may give you partial answers. In which case, ask the same question several times but in different phrasing until you feel you received the information to your satisfaction.

Remember that it cannot lie to you, but it can leave out information, which is why you ask in several ways.

Always do this part of the ritual to acknowledge or welcome the spirit. Remember, we are dealing with an entity and even though we have the control, we deal with this entity with respect.

We approach this summoning/calling in with love energy and truth, as well as command and authority.

We have to know that we are the connection to GOD/DIVINE POWER and that all spirits/entities coming to us were already tested and are in a positive energy space. So respect is due to them.

They are, after all, coming to answer your questions or to do your bidding.

<u>Payment</u>

When we ask a person to do something for us, such as doing a job, we normally pay them for their time and their work.

So it is in evocation. There is a payment to be made for the questions being answered or for the service being done for you. Sometimes for both.

It is important to pay the spirit, just as you would pay a person for services rendered.

Payment in any form is simply an exchange of energy. If you pay someone with money because they did a great job for you, you are exchanging energy.

Everything is made up of energy: You, the table, the clouds, and the sun. They simply vibrate at a different speed per second, which is what makes some objects look like they are solid.

So your payment to the spirit/entity that you summoned is an energy exchange that can be in various forms. You decide which form you want to give as payment. Whichever payment you choose, it can be the same each time or can always be different. You decide each time.

Some magicians/shamans decide what the payment will be from them prior to the evocation ritual. I recommend that you think of various forms that you are comfortable with before you do even your first evocation ritual. In this way, when the payment time comes, you don't have to think about it.

EVOCATION

You can go by what you "feel" or think is the best one for that particular situation.

Just as each job and person is different, so it is with spirit. You will have a sense, intuitively, of which form of energy exchange would be most pleasing to this spirit/entity. If you don't "feel" any particular one, then just go with the first form of payment that came into your mind. That will be the correct one.

Some of the payment forms that we can utilize are:

A Blessing

Dance

Music

Drumming

Poetry

Song

Love Energy

The Energy Technique

The strongest universal energy is LOVE. Therefore, if you simply visualize or think of love energy (usually "seen" as pink light, or you can visualize it as white) coming down from the universe through your crown chakra and flowing out of your palms or finger tips toward the spirit/entity, that is the simplest and most powerful payment. You will know when to stop because you will feel like you are done.

EVOCATION

The crown chakra is actually in a different place than we've been taught. Most martial artists and, of course, Adepts (Masters) and shamans all know this.

If you put your hand on top of your head, with the fingers pointing to the back of the head, and then take your other hand and place it at the back of your head, with the fingers pointing up, where the two hands meet is where your crown chakra is actually located.

Payment is very important in evocation. This does not mean that it is to be done in other rituals or other forms of magick. It is simply part of the evocation ritual and must be honored.

License to Depart

Since you summoned the spirit, it cannot leave without you giving it the license to depart.

Remember, you have all the control. You HAVE to send it back to whatever Realm it came from when you summoned it. Not doing so can be very dangerous to you.

In an authoritative manner, now say to the spirit/entity:

In the names of GOD, ADONAI and The Lord of Lords, because thou hast obeyed my commands, thou (_____) can go forth, as I now give thee license to depart. Now return to the Realm from which thou came at my calling. Be ready to come quickly and agreeably when next I call upon thee. May thee be Blessed by the Almighty GOD.

EVOCATION

Go now unto thine home in peace and do not cause harm to any human or living thing. Go forth and let there always be peace between thou and me, in the name of GOD, and be in readiness for when I summon thee again.

At this point, the one you summoned will depart. It has no choice but to do so. When next you summon the same one, the spirit will come from wherever the spirit is. Chains cannot bind this spirit. Oaths cannot hold the spirit. Nothing can stop this spirit from coming to you quickly and peaceably without delay.

The Closing

***Repeat the Banishing Ritual** once again to make sure the room or area is clear and the spirit/entity is gone and back to the Realm it was summoned from.

A **final step** is to open your arms wide to your sides at shoulder level and then bring them in to fold over your chest.

<u>#2</u>

EVOCATION

Next, if you are inside, open all the windows. You can burn incense at this time if you wish, but it is not needed. If you burn incense, I recommend these two protection incenses: Tobacco or Frankincense.

If you are wearing any ritual clothing, take them off and put them back in their place.

If you have magickal tools in the room or area, put them away now in their places.

I suggest at this time to ground yourself. You can do so by eating something. Do **not** drink anything very cold. You will feel like your body was shocked. It is not dangerous to you. It is simply uncomfortable.

Another grounding method is to think of white light lines of energy (like laser beams) going out of the bottom of your feet and into the center of the earth. Visualize a small ball, such as a baseball, in the earth's core. Next, wrap the lines around the ball to "hold" you there.

Make sure you feel grounded before going on with your daily life. You will be on the Beta brainwave level when you are back to dealing with this reality. Not on the Alpha/Theta brainwaves.

EVOCATION

SEALS/SIGILS/SYMBOLS

YOU don't absolutely need a sigil, symbol or seal to do the evocation rituals. However, if you so choose, make sure that you have the correct seal for the correct being you are going to summon.

You would take the symbol and place it on the floor or on the altar, if you are using one. It has to be next to you before you proceed with the evocation.

These symbols are a connection. They are a line of inter-dimensional energy. Think of them as a homing device or a beacon that connects to another realm.

It is as though you are on one end of the phone and the spirit or inter-dimensional being is at the other end. The symbol is the wire connecting you both.

Skill, ability and knowledge are of great importance and imperative in making the symbols. It is considered a Magickal Art.

So I have added some in this book that you can utilize. You don't need to make them yourself when so many are available in our time. Some symbols are on metal, some on wood and some on parchment or regular white paper, among other forms. The power is in the symbols themselves. Use them with discretion.

Sigils help us to connect to our inner and outer worlds. The symbols help us to communicate as we link both. They aid in connecting us with other Realms and intelligences.

We are setting up frequency waves through the Divine to connect us to whatever our Intent happens to be. The frequency will find and connect to the spirit/otherworldly being in any Realm so you can then proceed with the summoning.

Symbols are utilized to represent and connect through association with a physical or non-physical entity or situation.

This is a language of the mystic, shaman, magician and psychic. It is the language of the soul-mind. This is the universal language that everyone can understand. If you show a picture of a cat to anyone that has knowledge of what it is, they will immediately know what you mean, even without words. In the universal magickal language, all who are connected to that Higher Knowledge will understand.

A magician, shaman, and others who are in these spiritual/psychic/paranormal fields can also interpret them.

These sigils that we use have been passed down through the ages. You can start with these, knowing they are tried and true.

EVOCATION

First, pick one that fits your intent in your life at this moment. Then make a copy of it. The copy is the one you will be utilizing. You can use it more than once after you begin to work with the copy. That is because each sigil is unique in that it only connects to summoning one particular spirit/being. The more you can reuse the same copy, the more power it contains, and the connection after the first evocation will become quicker with time.

If you decide to use another copy, don't mistakenly worry that it will not work well. It is simply that you can gain a quicker connection by reusing the same copy.

THE SEALS

Archangel Metetron

Metetron is an Archangel. He has several names, some of which are: King of Angels, Chancellor of Heaven, King of the Whirlwinds, Chief of the Ministering Angels, the Lesser YHWH (the Tetragrammation).

Metetron is the connection between the Divine and man. Summon him if your intent is for connecting to Divine information or Healing. Call on Metetron in any form of book/record keeping to bring positivity, honesty and efficiency. (There are other reasons to call him, but start with these.)

 # 3

SEAL OF METATRON

EVOCATION

Angel Fortitude

Call on the Angel Fortitude when your intent is to heighten your courage and to endure adversity.

 # 4

The Second Pentacle of Jupiter

This seal is for gaining riches, honor, glory, tranquility, discovering treasure and getting past its guarding spirits as well as all good things. You can call on AB (Father), IHVH.

5

The First Pentacle of Venus

This seal is connected to spirits working with the energies of Venus, the Planet of Love. Angel names are Nogahiel, Acheliah, Socodiah, Nangariel.

 # 6

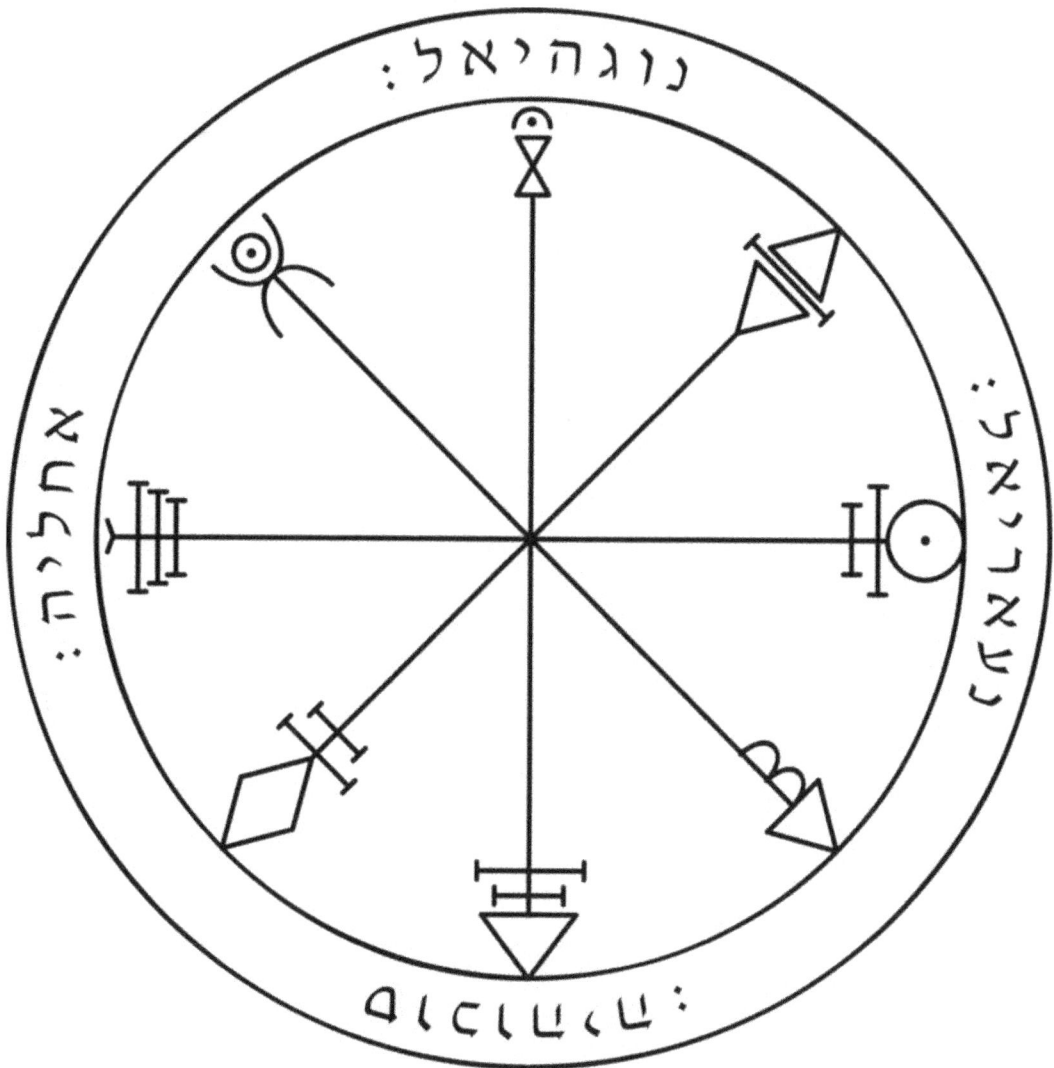

EVOCATION

The Fourth Pentacle of Mercury

This seal helps you to gain knowledge and understanding of all created things. Helps you to seek and understand hidden things. Summon the spirits called Allatori.

#7

The Fourth Pentacle of the Moon

This seal protects you from all evil to your body or soul. You can gain knowledge of all herbs and of stones. Summon the Angels Sophiel and Yahel. Summon also the Divine Name, EHEIEH ASHER EHEIEH.

8

EVOCATION

<u>CONCLUSION</u>

IT seems like there should be more to it. Right? Well, there is. There are evocation rituals that are more complex, as well as others that are simpler. There is also another part you can add on to this ritual, but you would need to be able to perform this version perfectly first.

Do not misunderstand me...Adding on to the ritual does *not* give you better results. It is simply another version.

Our general outlook aligns like this:

East relates to Life; South relates to Light; West relates to Love; North relates to Law

The need for skill can never be overestimated.

The aim is to make your magickal life easier and to elevate you to a Higher Level of spirituality.

You have to make sure all is in place. You have to know by heart what to do before entering into the evocation.

Remember to come to the evocation with a pure Intent in your heart.

Do not take this lightly, as it is not a game.

Go forth, find and become the magick.

<u>YES YOU CAN!!!</u>

EVOCATION

If you enjoyed this book, send your name and mailing address for our FREE catalog.

Global Communications

P.O. Box 753

New Brunswick, NJ 08903

Email: mrufo8@hotmail.com

www.conspiracyjournal.com

SPELLCRAFT, WISECRAFT, OCCULT, METAPHYSICS
Workbooks And Study Guides
From Qualified Instructors

MARIA D' ANDREA

Maria is a gifted psychic, spiritual counselor, and shaman. She has helped those in matters of luck, love and financial concerns. She lectures, holds workshops and does private counseling in NY area. Her books are exclusively published by Tim Beckley.

HEAVEN SENT MONEY SPELLS
IMAGINE RECEIVING MONEY JUST BY USING THE POWERS OF YOUR MIND! Let Maria D' Andrea Tell You How To Turn Your Dreams Into Cash — And Become A Virtual Human MONEY MAGNET. Inspired by the Heavenly Light. Here are spells that anyone can learn to execute. Use herbs, candles and gemstones to create prosperity! Have talismans and amulets help do the work for you!
8.5x11—Workbook format—132 pages—ISBN-13: 978-1606111000—$19.95

SECRET OCCULT GALLERY AND SPELL CASTING FORMULARY
COME UP TO THE "GOOD LIFE" with Maria's top dozen enchantments and occult gallery of mystical and spiritual essentials. Easy to perform spells that could put you on easy street.
8.5x11—Workbook format—152 pages—ISBN-13: 978-1606111284—$21.95

YOUR PERSONAL MEGA POWER SPELLS
A valuable interpretation of blessings, protections, hex-breaking rituals and ceremonies as practiced by the most ardent of Wiccans, alchemists, sages and occultists down through the centuries.
8.5X11—252 pages—ISBN-13: 978-1606111055—$21.95

SECRET MAGICAL ELIXIRS OF LIFE
Explore The Paranormal Vibrations Of Crystals, Gems And Stones For Good Health, Enhanced Psychic Powers And Phenomenal Inner Strength!
8.5X11—150 PAGES—ISBN-13: 978-1606111147—$21.95

HOW TO ELIMINATE ANXIETY AND STRESS THROUGH THE OCCULT
Just utilize Crystals, Gemstones, Meditation, Herbs, Oils, Visualization, Chakras, Music, Prayer, Mandalas, Mantras, Incense, Candles and More.
6x9—150 pages—ISBN-13: 978-1606111383—$19.95

MYSTICAL, MAGICKAL BEASTS AND BEINGS
Come explore the supernatural side of man's best – and worst – "friends" as related in the strangest stories involving beasties of all sorts – seen and unseen. And uppermost learn how to get them to assist in our lives in a positive way. Other contributors include Penny Melis and Sean Casteel.
8.5x11—224 pages—ISBN-13: 978-1606111567—$21.95

OCCULT GRIMORIE AND MAGICAL FORMULARY
10 BOOKS ROLLED INTO ONE! – OVER 500 SPELLS! Reveals the secret of the ages. Manifest your destiny NOW! Most powerful spellcasters deliberately leave out important information. NOT MARIA!
8.5x11—236 pages—ISBN-13: 978-1606111086—$24.00

SUPER SPECIAL: Retail customers get all of Maria's books as listed for $139.00 + $15.00 Postage/Shipping. FREE DVD WITH 3 OF MARIA'S BOOKS OR MORE